BRASS IN COLOR

Five-Note Scale Studies

TRUMPET

BOOK TWO

by Sean Burdette

This book belongs to
_____

ISBN 13: 978-1-949670-48-6
Copyright © 2020 BRASS IN COLOR, LLC
All Rights Reserved.

Any duplication, adaptation or arrangement of the compositions, tablature design and illustrations contained in this collection and series requires the written consent of the publisher. Unauthorized uses are an infringement of the U.S. Copyright Act and are punishable by law.

Introduction

Welcome to Brass in Color Scale Studies!

Brass in Color scale studies for trumpet is a seven-book series that introduces students to five-note and one-octave scales. Brass in Color scale studies also introduce students to scale patterns, etudes and the use of key signatures written in major and minor keys.

What is a scale?

A music scale is a series of notes organized by half steps and whole steps. A music scale gets its name from the first note of the scale. If a scale starts with the note **C** it will be a type of **C Scale**. The organization of notes by half steps and whole steps tells students whether the scale is a **C Major Scale** or a **C Minor Scale**.

Why practice scales?

Practicing music scales is a basic exercise that helps students develop the ability to play easily and accurately. Playing scales also allows students to practice a variety of techniques such as articulations (slurring and tonguing) and dynamics (loud and soft) that are used when playing music.

Using the Brass in Color Scale Studies

Each book in this series uses a color-coded tablature (Color Fingerings) to help students learn the proper fingerings for each note of the scale. Students can review these fingerings using the chart to the right or by using the expanded fingering chart in the back of this book (pp. 28-29).

There are seven different fingering combinations for the trumpet.

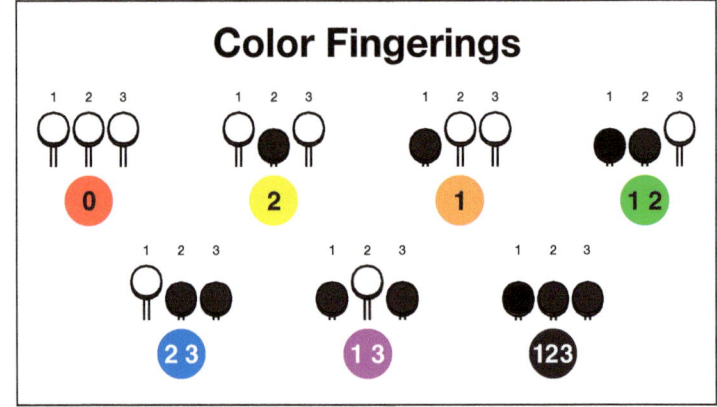

Five-Note Scales, Scale Patterns and Etudes

There are three sections in each scale studies book. Students can check off their progress after finishing the exercises in each section. In the first section students identity the letter name for each note of the scale while practicing the correct fingerings using the color-coded tablature. Students then play the scale using different articulation techniques. Finally, the student should learn to play the scale from memory. In the second section students practice scale patterns using the notes of the five-note scale. In the third section students practice etudes (melodic and technical studies) based on each five-note scale.

Contents

1 Scales

E♭ Major	 4		E Minor	 7
F♯ Minor	 4		D♭ Major	 7
E Major	 5		C♯ Major	 8
C♯ Minor	 5		G♭ Minor	 8
F♯ Major	 6		F Major	 9
A♭ Major	 6		F Minor	 9

2 Scale Patterns

E♭ Major	 10		E Minor	 16
F♯ Minor	 11		D♭ Major	 17
E Major	 12		C♯ Major	 18
C♯ Minor	 13		G♭ Minor	 19
F♯ Major	 14		F Major	 20
A♭ Major	 15		F Minor	 21

3 Etudes

E♭ Major	 22		E Minor	 25
F♯ Minor	 22		D♭ Major	 25
E Major	 23		C♯ Major	 26
C♯ Minor	 23		G♭ Minor	 26
F♯ Major	 24		F Major	 27
A♭ Major	 24		F Minor	 27

Fingering Chart 28

Scales

E♭ Major

Name the notes of the scale ▶

Practice the fingerings for the scale ▶   2 3 1 0 2 3 1

Play the scale: ☐ Tongued ☐ Slurred ☐ From Memory

F♯ Minor

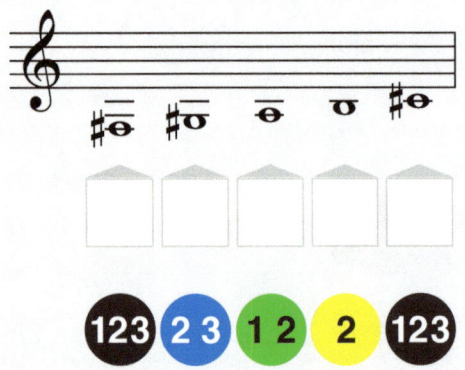

Name the notes of the scale ▶

Practice the fingerings for the scale ▶   123 2 3 1 2 2 123

Play the scale: ☐ Tongued ☐ Slurred ☐ From Memory

Scales

E Major

Name the notes of the scale ▶

Practice the fingerings for the scale ▶

Play the scale: ☐ Tongued ☐ Slurred ☐ From Memory

C♯ Minor

Name the notes of the scale ▶

Practice the fingerings for the scale ▶

Play the scale: ☐ Tongued ☐ Slurred ☐ From Memory

Scales

F♯ Major

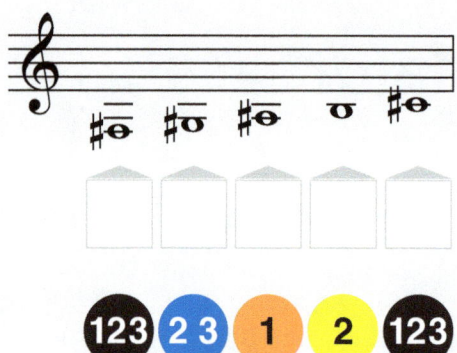

Name the notes of the scale ▶

Practice the fingerings for the scale ▶

Play the scale: ☐ Tongued   ☐ Slurred   ☐ From Memory

A♭ Major

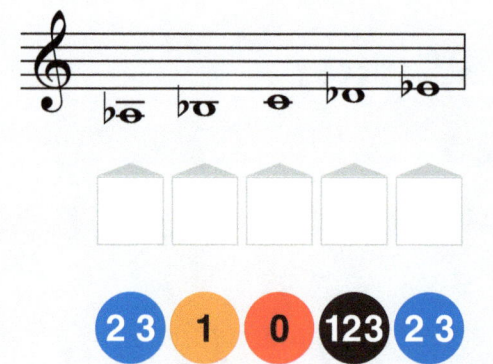

Name the notes of the scale ▶

Practice the fingerings for the scale ▶

Play the scale: ☐ Tongued   ☐ Slurred   ☐ From Memory

Scales

E Minor

Name the notes of the scale ▸

Practice the fingerings for the scale ▸

Play the scale: ☐ Tongued ☐ Slurred ☐ From Memory

D♭ Major

Name the notes of the scale ▸

Practice the fingerings for the scale ▸

Play the scale: ☐ Tongued ☐ Slurred ☐ From Memory

Brass in Color

Scales

C♯ Major

Name the notes of the scale ▶

Practice the fingerings for the scale ▶

Play the scale: ☐ Tongued   ☐ Slurred   ☐ From Memory

G♭ Major

Name the notes of the scale ▶

Practice the fingerings for the scale ▶

Play the scale: ☐ Tongued   ☐ Slurred   ☐ From Memory

Brass in Color

Scales

F Major

Name the notes of the scale ▶

Practice the fingerings for the scale ▶

Play the scale: ☐ Tongued ☐ Slurred ☐ From Memory

F Minor

Name the notes of the scale ▶

Practice the fingerings for the scale ▶

Play the scale: ☐ Tongued ☐ Slurred ☐ From Memory

Brass in Color

Scale Patterns

E♭ Major

Pattern 1 Completed ☐

Pattern 2 Completed ☐

Pattern 3 Completed ☐

Pattern 4 Completed ☐

F# Minor

Scale Patterns

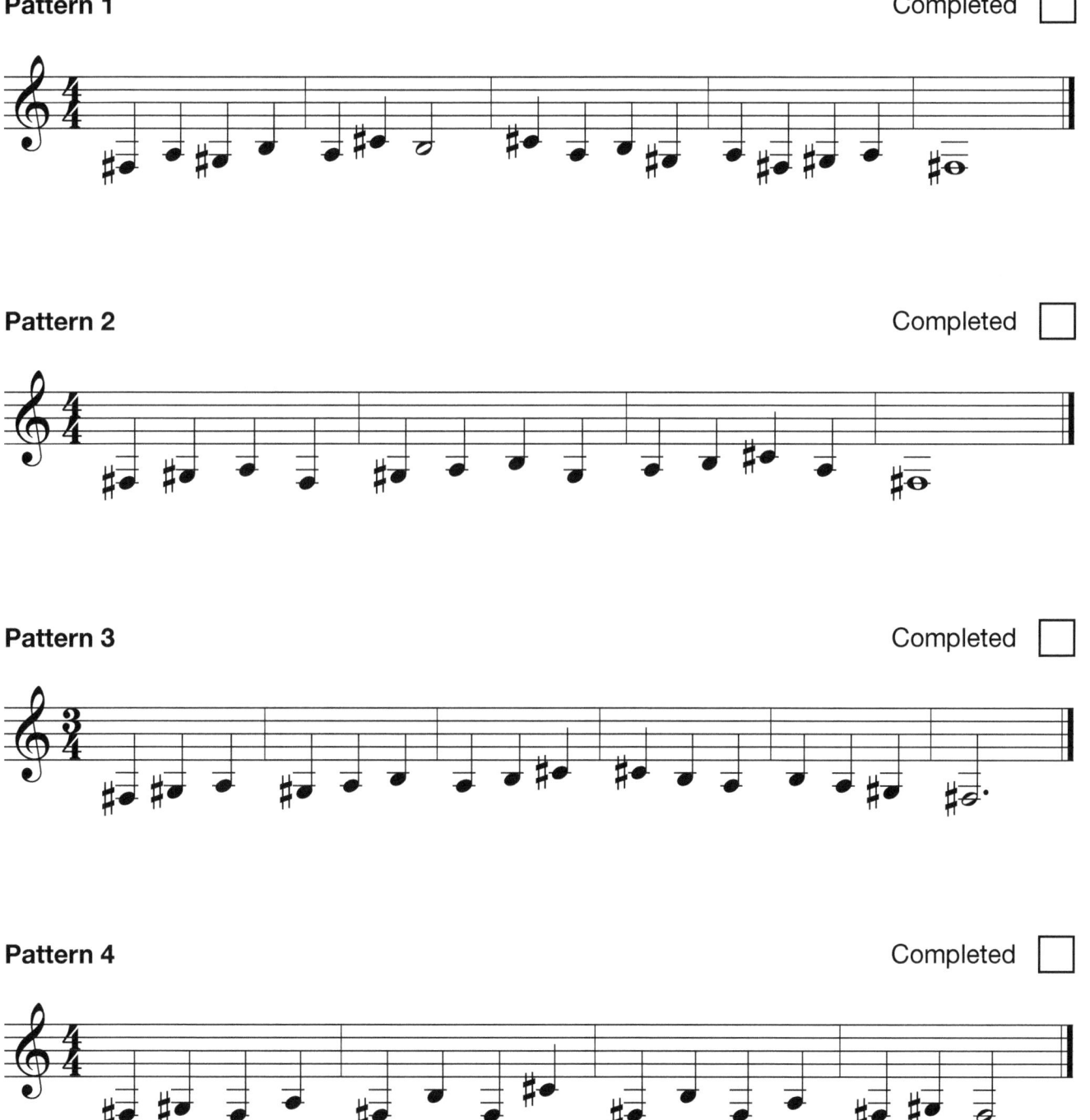

Scale Patterns

E Major

Pattern 1   Completed ☐

Pattern 2   Completed ☐

Pattern 3   Completed ☐

Pattern 4   Completed ☐

Scale Patterns

F# Major

Pattern 1   Completed ☐

Pattern 2   Completed ☐

Pattern 3   Completed ☐

Pattern 4   Completed ☐

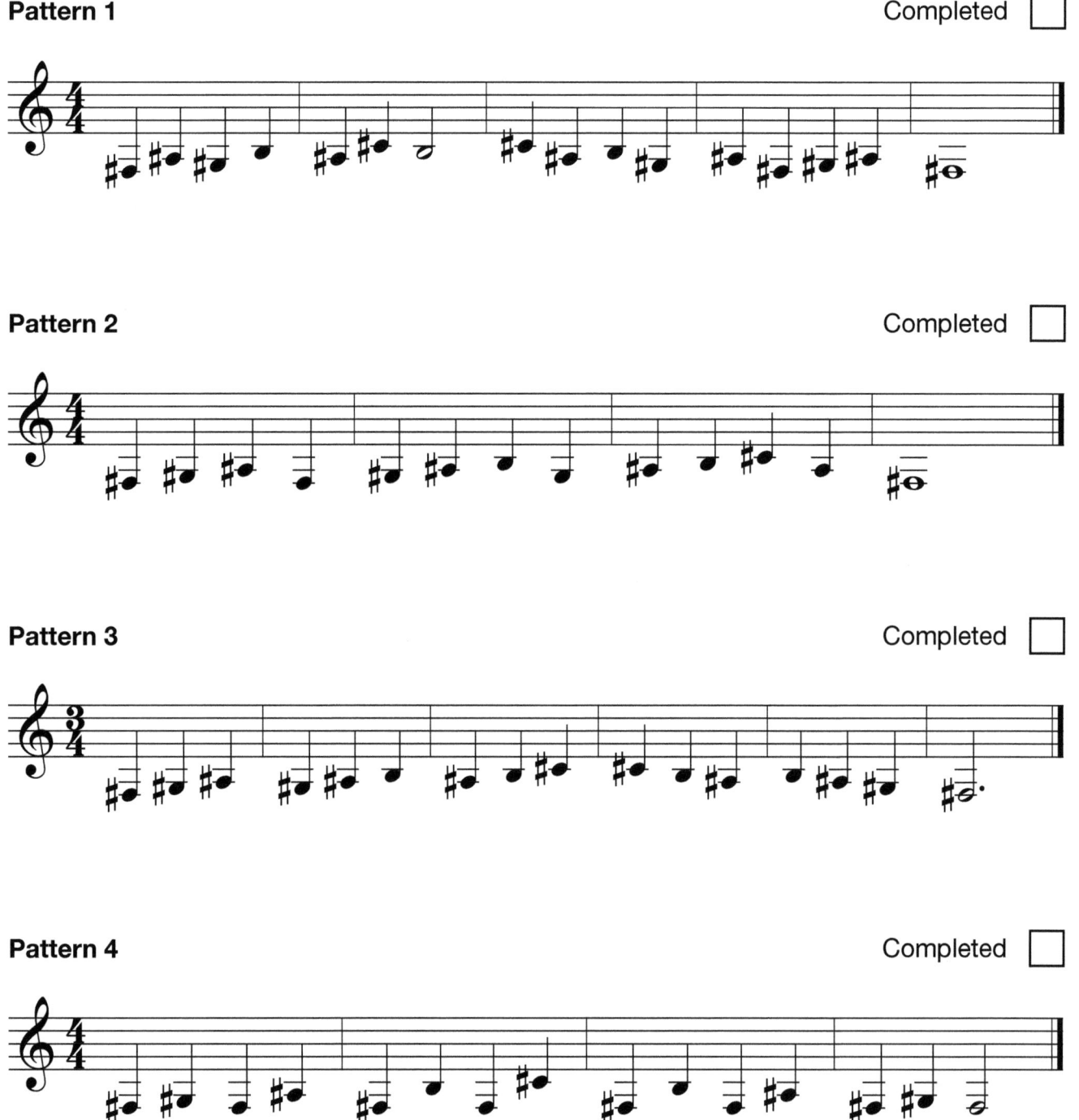

A♭ Major

Scale Patterns

Pattern 1 — Completed ☐

Pattern 2 — Completed ☐

Pattern 3 — Completed ☐

Pattern 4 — Completed ☐

Scale Patterns

E Minor

D♭ Major

Scale Patterns

Pattern 1 — Completed ☐

Pattern 2 — Completed ☐

Pattern 3 — Completed ☐

Pattern 4 — Completed ☐

Brass in Color

Scale Patterns

C# Major

Pattern 1 Completed ☐

Pattern 2 Completed ☐

Pattern 3 Completed ☐

Pattern 4 Completed ☐

G♭ Major

Scale Patterns

Pattern 1 — Completed ☐

Pattern 2 — Completed ☐

Pattern 3 — Completed ☐

Pattern 4 — Completed ☐

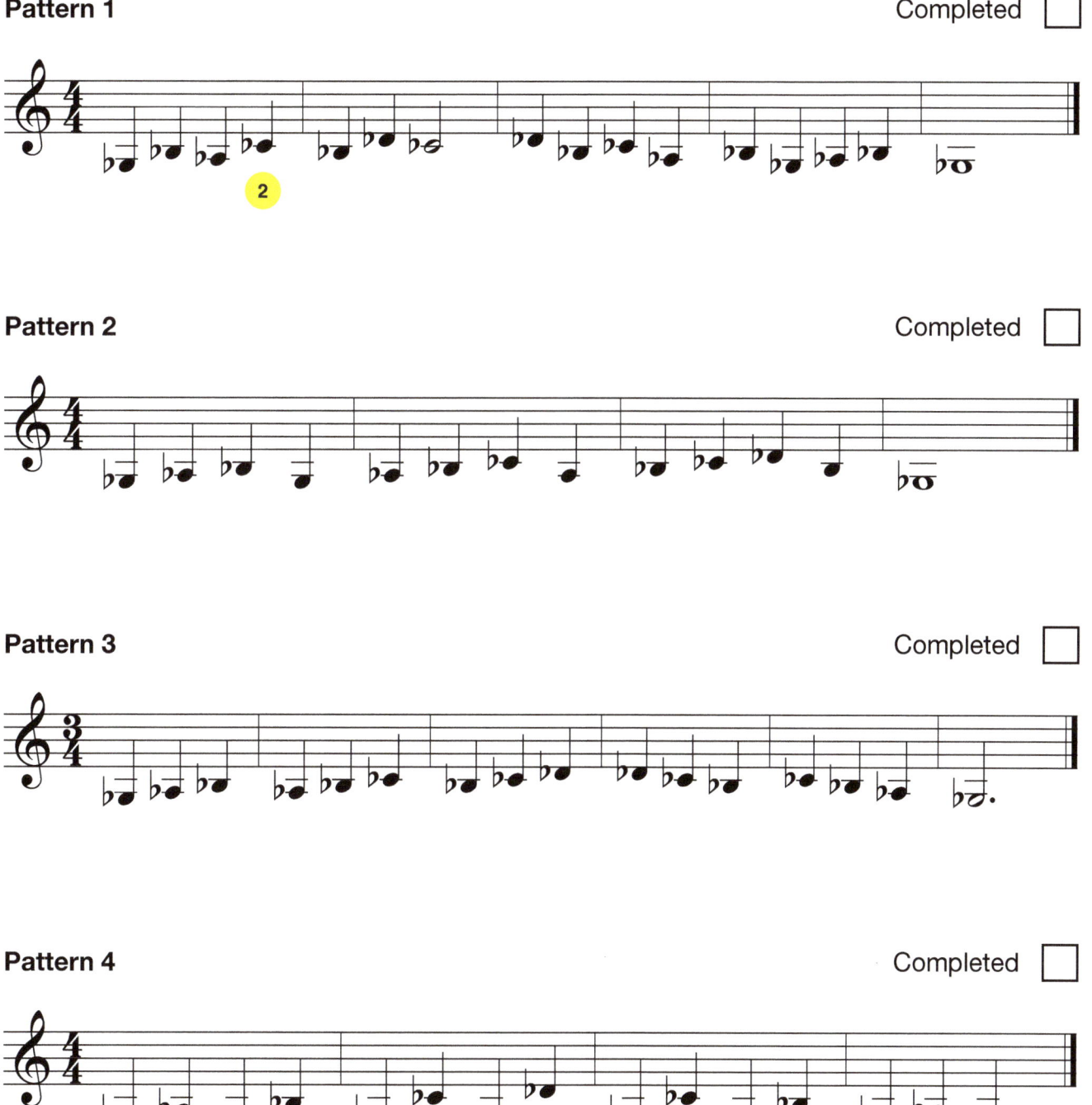

Brass in Color

Scale Patterns

F Major

Pattern 1   Completed ☐

Pattern 2   Completed ☐

Pattern 3   Completed ☐

Pattern 4   Completed ☐

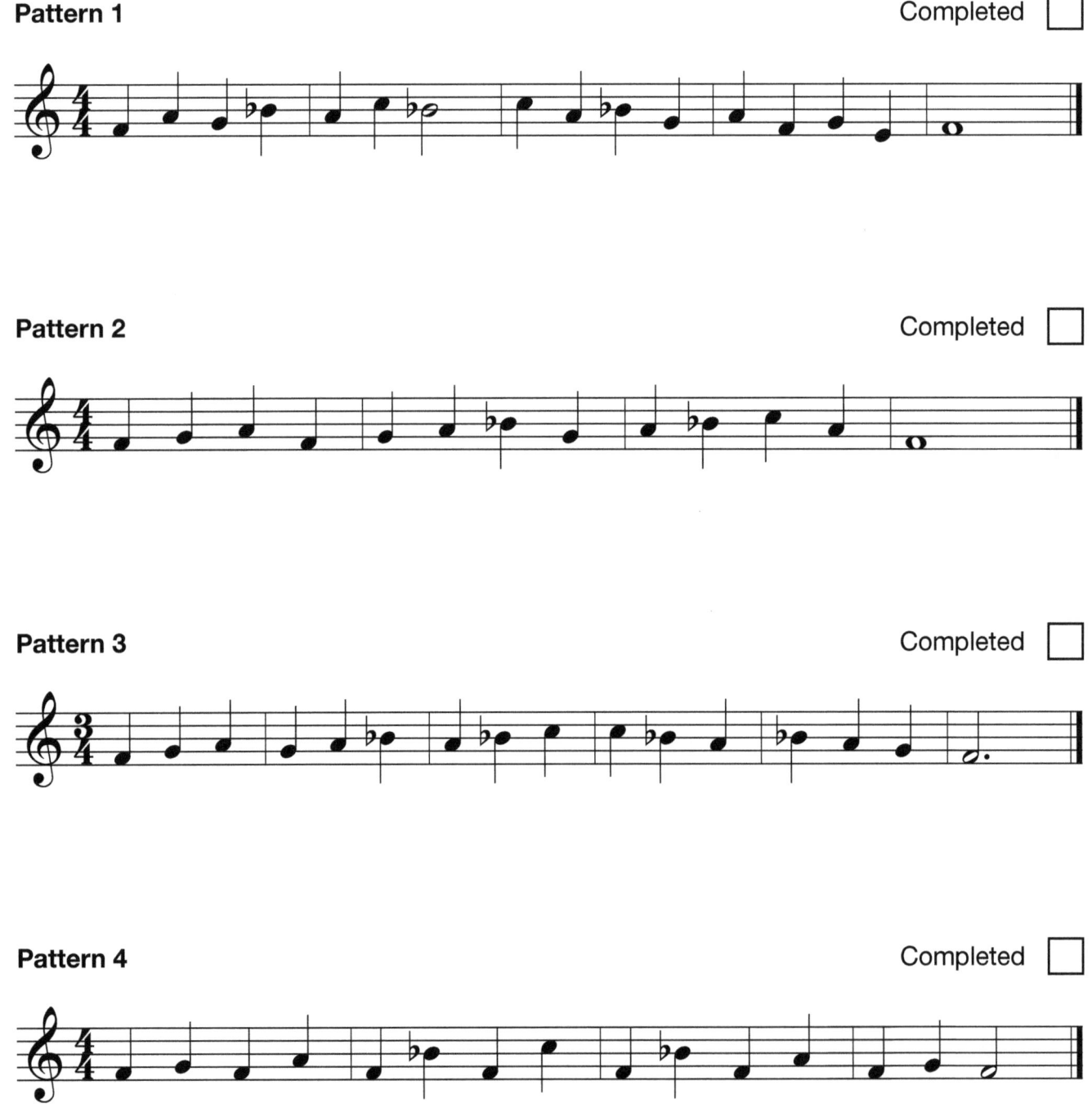

F Minor

Pattern 1   Completed ☐

Pattern 2   Completed ☐

Pattern 3   Completed ☐

Pattern 4   Completed ☐

Scale Patterns

Brass in Color

Etudes

E♭ Major

Completed ☐

F♯ Minor

Completed ☐

Etudes

E Major

Completed ☐

C♯ Minor

Completed ☐

Brass in Color

Etudes

F♯ Major

Completed ☐

A♭ Major

Completed ☐

Etudes

E Minor

Completed ☐

D♭ Major

Completed ☐

Etudes

C♯ Major

Completed ☐

G♭ Major

Completed ☐

Etudes

F Major

Completed ☐

F Minor

Completed ☐

Brass in Color

Fingering Chart

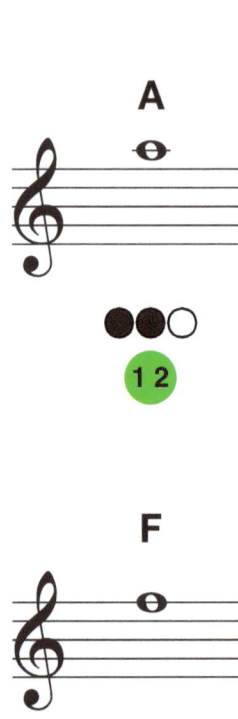

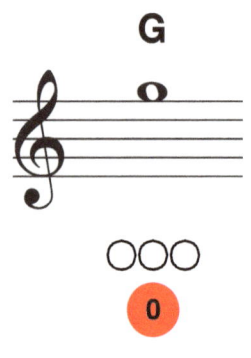

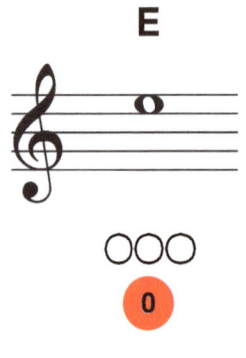
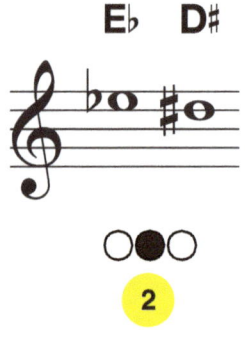
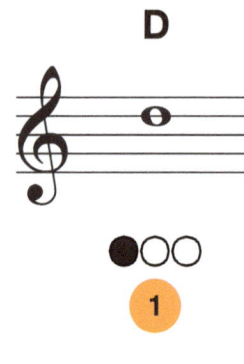

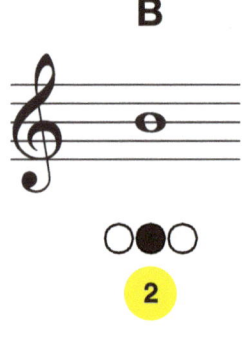

Brass in Color

Fingering Chart

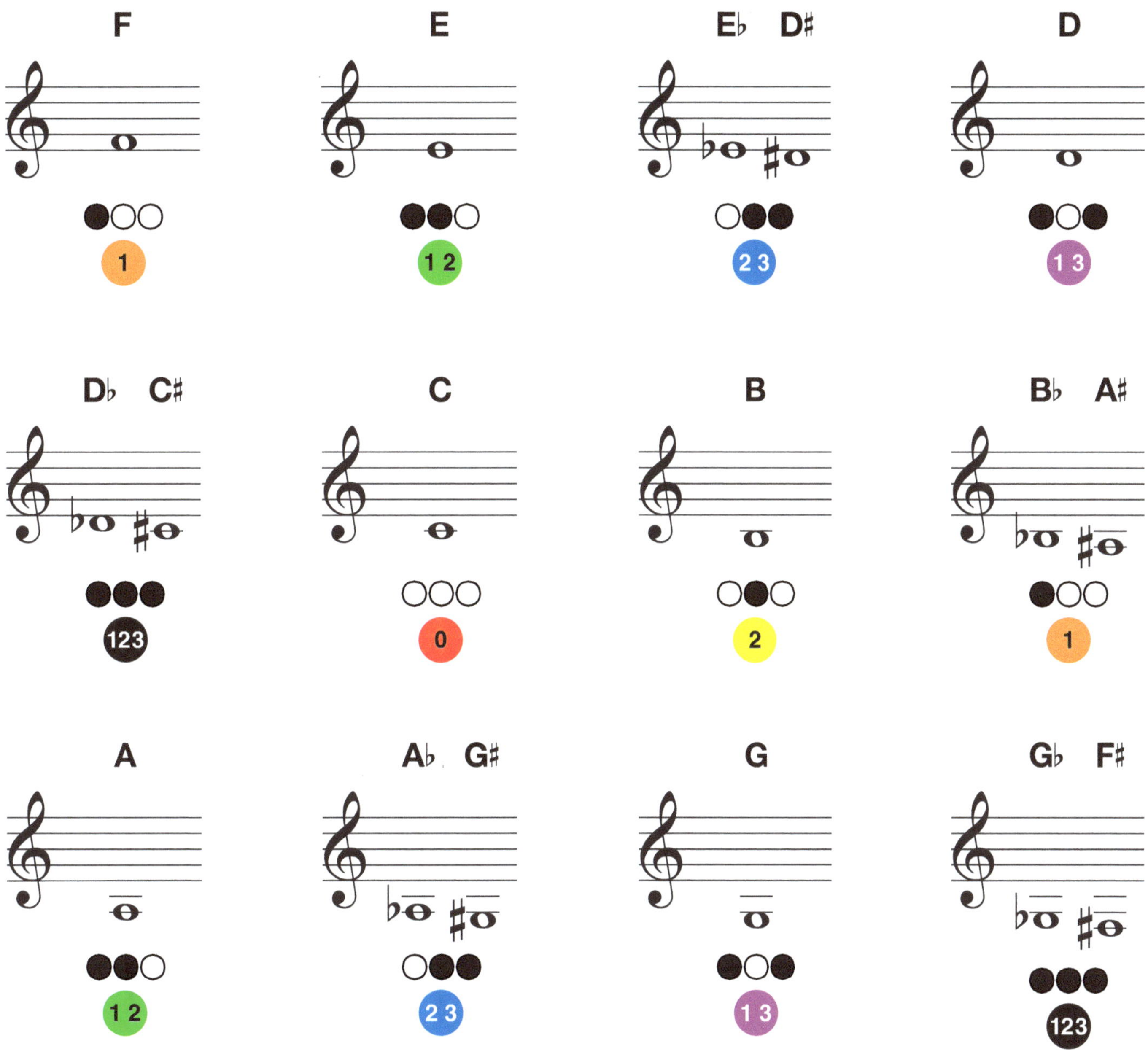

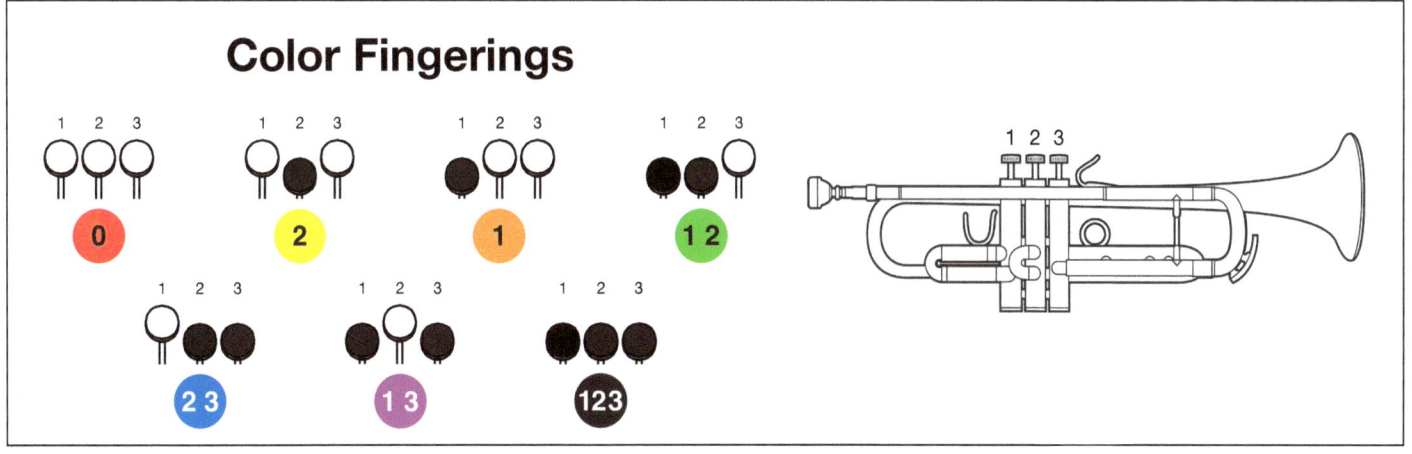

Books

SCALE STUDIES BOOKS 1-3 introduce students to five-note scales, scale patterns and etudes written in major and minor keys.

SCALE STUDIES BOOKS 4-7 introduce students to one-octave scales, scale patterns, etudes written in major and minor keys using key signatures.